Christ and the Laborer

Our Lord Appears to Charles J. Grestl in
the Mohawk Valley, Where the Church
Militant is Strong

M. Virginia Southworth

D1282059

For Doris Goff, the niece of Charles Grestl and, a prayer warrior for the unborn. She fought fearlessly for the sanctity of life to be upheld.

Doris Bach Goff (1929 – 2022)

"Before I formed you in the womb, I knew you. And before you were born, I consecrated you; I have appointed you the prophet of the nations."

1 Jeremiah 1:5

Chapters:

I

Charles Grestl

Charles J. Grestl was born in Utica, New York in 1886. He married Lena Neyenhousein in 1907. Although Mr. and Mrs. Grestl did not have children of their own, they shared their lives with the young people of Utica. They were affectionately known as "Aunt Lena and Uncle Charlie" to the local boy scouts and to the children at St. John's Orphanage.

Charles J. Grestl

One day, in the Spring of 1947, Mr. Grestl went to visit his wife in the hospital. He had accompanied her regularly for her daily radium treatments. Now she lay dying of cancer in the St. Elizabeth Hospital in Utica, New York.

St. Elizabeth Hospital Utica, New York

In the afternoon, Mr. Grestl returned to work. Mr. Grestl was employed at the Oneida Knitting Mills on Broad Street in Utica. He was the foreman.

Knitting Mill in West Utica

He was at his desk when suddenly,
he was taken from there to the

place where he used to live. He was transported to a location on Flanagan Road at the southwestern base of the Adirondack Mountains.

II

The Encounter

He found himself walking up a hill, but he stopped as he could not go any farther. There were boulders, stumps of trees, and old barbed wire.

Then, he heard a voice. Charles turned and saw Our Lord and Savior Jesus Christ.

"Hello son, come over here and sit down."

This was his first apparition of Christ. It was accompanied by a bright light. Mr. Grestl knew then that he was speaking with Christ.

Our Lord was whittling beautiful
angels out of wood.

They had a discussion. How long, Charles could not say. This is how Our Lord explained why the road was blocked:

"This is as far as you have got with your good works in life." Jesus told Charles.

Mrs. Grestl died shortly after.

St. Anne and Blessed Mother Mary as a young girl.

Charles met Jesus again about one month later. The road was

cleared about four feet more from where he stood before.

Charles was to see Our Lord twelve more times over the course of several months.

In one of these visits, Jesus asked Charles to go to his Pastor, the late Father Collins. He was to ask him to make an appointment for Charles to meet with Bishop Foery of Syracuse, New York.

Jesus requested that the bishop have a medal struck with the figure of Christ Himself and a laborer.

III

The Messenger

Charles did as he was told. The Pastor and the Bishop both referred to Charles as a "messenger."

On another visit, Jesus asked Charles to have Bishop Walter Foery of Syracuse write to Francis Cardinal Spellman of New York for an interview.

After the interview took place, His Eminence told Mr. Grestl that he would relay his incredible encounters and story with the Holy Father, Pope Pius XII.

Pope John XXIII

Letter to Pope John XXIII

March 8, 1961

Your Most Holy Father, Pope John
XXIII:

I, your most humble servant, Charles
Grestl, am writing you now to ask if you
have run across a message concerning
my story which Cardinal Spellman
brought to the late Holy Father, Pope
Pius XII.

The story, where in 1947, I had met with
the foothills of the Adirondack
Mountains – Christ Himself. Not a
dream, but at the daylight hour of about
11:30 A.M. the last of April, 1947. My
wife, at that time, was dying from cancer
in St Elizabeth's Hospital, Utica, New
York.

I used to go up to the hospital to take my
wife down to the basement for radium
treatments to kill the pain. She thought
she had arthritis, but the doctor told me

she would last only 3 to 4 weeks as she had cancer. After coming back one of those visits at the hospital, sitting at my desk in the factory where I was a foreman, I was taken from my place of business back to the place where I used to live. I could feel the warmth of the sunshine and the breezes, so I know I was not asleep. I met folks going in the opposite direction and I said to them, "Come along with me, I'm going for a hike in the country." At that time, I didn't know my destination, but it led me to this road out of the country which they now call the foothills of the Adirondack Mountains, about one mile from the Mohawk River. This is the same river the Shrine of Martyrs of Auriesville is on, about 60 miles from Utica, my hometown.

On my way to this place, I passed farms where I used to work, weeding, when I was a youngster. The cows in the pasture where I used to work on the farm looked so clear and bright that particular day. Just above this farm on that road, there is a night-club and on the other side of the road there is a slaughterhouse. In between there is a hill, where the road turns and goes up to a place they call

"Flanagan's Old Home." Starting up the hill, I only got about four feet up the hill, when, to my surprise, I was stopped by boulders, stumps of trees, and old barbed wire. I scratched my head and said to myself, isn't it strange – a beautiful day for a hike in the country, and I can't go any further." Then a voice said "Hello, Son," and I didn't turn but I knew the Voice – why, I can never tell you. I said "Hello, Master." He said, "Come over here and sit down." On the side of the road there was bench he was sitting on. His clothes were made of all that was around – the twigs, the grass, no cloth. His hands, His feet, His face were flesh and His hair was as the sand banks behind Him. The bench on which He sat was of the same materials as His garb. He said "Son, sit down." He said, "You wonder why you can't go any further." I said, "Yes, Master, I was out for a hike on this beautiful day, and I can't go any further." He said, "Son, this is as far as You've got with good works in life." Just then a beautiful light appeared over the hill where this road would have led me to. I've never seen such a beautiful bright light. And I said, "What's that light, my Master." "That's my Father's House." I said, "Oh, yes, in my Father's House there are many mansions." He said, "Son, go back to the city from whence you came and work amongst your fellow men as you have been doing. Each time you come back; you'll see the path will be cleared further upon the way to my Father's House."

At one time, I had 100 boys in a Scout Troop, and another troop at the Children's Hospital. I had 4 or 5 groups of boys at the Orphan Home. I was President of our Holy Name Society; Vice-President of our Legion of Mary. I have been President of the First Saturday Group of

Our Lady of Fatima. From that time on, I was in ecstasy – for one month. I did my work – it must have been all right for I had no complaints – I ate and slept as usual, but I seemed to be out of this world. How much time I spent with the Master; I cannot tell. I know I was with Him at least 12 times. The second time I went back I could see He had moved about 4 feet from where He was before. I knew because the shavings were in a circle around the bench because He had been carving when I met Him the first time. This time He picked up a piece of wood about one foot long and three inches through. Handing it to me with also a carver's knife that curved towards the end, he said, "Son, cut the bark off this wood for this is what He was doing when I first met Him – carving beautiful angels out of wood. He said, "Son, I learned this is at my Father's carpenter shop." He said "Son, the priests represent me and on the altar I'm always waiting." He said, "Son, live as you've been living, and people will believe you when you tell them this story."

The third time, after sitting down on the bench with the Master, I picked up the wood and started cutting the bark off. I looked down to see if I couldn't see the imprint in the Master's foot or in the Master's hand but in one hand he held the wood, and in the other, the knife he was carving with. But, on His left foot, I could see the imprint of the nail. He said, "Son, go to your pastor and ask him to get an appointment for you with Bishop Foery of Syracuse, N.Y. You tell the Bishop that Christ wants a medal struck with the figure of Christ Himself and a laborer." I was cutting the bark off the wood, and He was carving the images from the wood, and to have a scapular made with the same picture on, also pamphlets printed with the same picture, also to have pamphlets distributed to all the nations on earth. I said to the Master, "Bishop Foery will say to me, I don't know you, Mr. Grestl, and Christ said, "You don't know the Bishop like I know him." I asked, "Master, how could the pamphlets be distributed?" He said, "There's a machine flies so high it's over No Man's Land but my Father's land." I went to see my pastor, the late Father Collins, and I explained to him what the Master wanted. He said, "Son, you are a messenger, I'll get in touch with the Bishop as soon as I can."

I received word to come to Syracuse from the Bishop. The Bishop asked, "Mr. Grestl, what's the story?" and I explained to him what Christ had told me. One thing I had to repeat about three times, what the Master had said: "Son, the priests represent me on the altar and I'm always waiting," and also that He had learned to carve the images in His father's shop. He, the Bishop, looked at me for quite some time. He said, "Mr. Grestl, I believe you – I really believe you are a messenger. We will have to do a lot of praying for there will be more to come.

I said to the Bishop: "My wife is dying in the hospital." He said he had 5 priests ill in the same hospital and that he would drop in and see my wife, which he did, and prayed over her for about 15 minutes.

Sometime after, at one of my other meetings with the Master, He had given the Bishop time to do something about the medal, the scapular, and the pamphlets, all before the Korean situation and all the labor troubles we had and are still having today. If every man could have been wearing the medal, using Christ as their champion, we wouldn't be having such troubles yet. At the next meeting with Christ, He said: "Go to your pastor and ask your pastor to get permission from the Bishop to write to Cardinal Spellman of New York for an interview with you and to the Cardinal and tell him the same story you told the Bishop Foery of Syracuse." My pastor said he would, and a short time after he phoned that he had received permission and was writing to New York for an interview for me with Cardinal Spellman.

In the meantime, my wife died. Everybody said I must have been happy because I was smiling all the while the night she died. I couldn't get a priest for her, though there were three priests at the parish house. They were all out on sick calls, and the Chaplain at the hospital was in attendance on another person in the hospital dying at the same time as my wife. So I had to say the prayers for the dying for my wife. The next night after the funeral, I met a man outside of our church. He said, "Are you Mr. Grestl." I said, "Yes." He said, "You are in boy's work, aren't you?." I told him of my two Scout troops and the troop I had at the Orphan Home. He said he would like to get into boy's work. He had just returned from China where he had spent 9 years as Secretary to the Bishop Ford of Maryknoll.

So, I received word to come to New York City. My pastor said, "Now, this is serious." But I took this gentleman, a Mr. Boyd with me, thinking they would be interested in him, coming out of China where the Communists were just getting in. So, I took him to New York City with me. We were met at the door of the Cardinal's residence by the Cardina's secretary, a Father Murphy. He invited us in – we sat down and introduced ourselves. He said, "Mr. Grestl, what's the story?" I repeated just the same as I had told my pastor and the Bishop of Syracuse. I had to repeat what the Master said, "the priests represent me and I'm always waiting on the altar" and about Christ's work in his father's carpenter shop to learn the carving. The secretary told me that the Cardinal was not at home but in Australia at that time, but he said when the Cardinal returns, I'll give him your story. I returned to my home 250 miles from New York City.

Sometime after my pastor phoned me, around 10 P.M., and said Bishop Foery called him from Rochester where the next day he was to meet with Cardinal Spellman. He inquired if there was anything else I wanted to add to the story. I told him "No, but Christ wanted the message delivered to the Cardinal and not to his secretary". My pastor said that he would phone the bishop and tell him that. One week later, I received a letter from Cardinal Spellman, telling me to come to New York. I took the same man, Mr. Boyd, with me and Cardinal Spellman met us at the door. We were invited in. We knelt and kissed his ring. He blessed us, and asked us to sit down, and he asked, "Mr. Grestl, what is the story?" So, I told him the same as I had told his secretary. I had to repeat about what Christ said, "the priests represent me and I'm always waiting on the altar" and that Christ was taught in His father's carpenter's shop to carve.

The Cardinal looked at me for about 10 minutes. He said, "Mr. Grestl, I believe you. I'm making my report to Rome, and I'll bring your story to Pope Pius XII, the Holy Father." That was in 1947. November 1949, I had a cancer and was to be operated on in the same hospital where my wife died from cancer. The night before the operation, I awoke about 1:30 A.M. and heard my name called. I shook my head and sat up in bed, it sounded far away – it kept coming nearer and nearer and the closer it came, the sweeter the voice. Then someone held my hand and the voice said "You wouldn't think me a very good

28

Mother not to come to you at this time. I have a lot of work for you to do." By that time, I knew it was Our Lady. Our Lady said her visit to me had nothing to do with Her Son's visit with me in 1947. But when that's approved, will you have them say my Rosary at that devotion."

So, I had to go to my pastor to inquire what She meant. He explained that someday, if it's taken out of just a private revelation and through some miracle, it becomes an approved shrine, the site where the revelation took place, that She would like to have Her rosary said at the devotions. Each morning after receiving the Body and Blood of Christ at the Sacrifice of the Mass, Our Lady takes me by the hand. Her mother, St. Anne, takes me by the other hand, with St. Joseph, St. John, St. Michael, {my guardian angel}, and St. Peter, we go to the throne of the Holy Ghost. I say to the Holy Ghost, "I am here with those who love you, and I love you too, but I am a sinner amongst them. Please give me the graces and blessings to carry me through this world of flesh and the devil."

He blesses me and puts out His hand for me to kiss His Hand and says to me "Come to the Master." Then we leave and go to the throne of Christ and at the throne of Christ, I say the same thing. I am here with those who love you, Master, and I love you too, but I am a sinner amongst them. Please give me your graces and blessings to carry me through against the world, the flesh, and the devil." Christ blesses me, puts out His hand, I kiss the spot the nail was driven in, and He says, "Come to my Father." We leave and go to the Father's throne. I say again, "I am with those who love you and I love you too, but I am a sinner amongst them. Please give me the blessings against the world, the flesh, and the devil." He gives me His blessings. 'He puts out His hand. I kiss it. I say, "In the name of the Father, the Son, and the Holy Ghost~ I thank you, Father."

Then I'm back in my pew again – that happened each day from 1947 to 1961. There are many more things to tell, too many to write down. Maybe someday, sitting at your feet, I could explain many things that only you, Most Holy Father, could understand: If this is approved,

Our Lady would like the name of the Shrine, "Christ the King."

Respectfully yours,

your Humble Servant,

CHARLES J. GRESTL

St. John

IV

A Lady Comes to Visit

Two years later in November of 1949, Charles was diagnosed with cancer. He was in the hospital waiting to have his surgery. The night prior to his surgery, at 1:30 a.m., he was taken aback on hearing a sweet voice call his name. This prompted Charles to sit straight up in bed. Standing in front of him, was Our Blessed Mother. She held Charles's hand to comfort him. Our Lady told Charles that this visit was unrelated to the visits from her Son in 1947. However, She did request that when approval is given for the shrine to be erected at the place where Jesus visited him, that It be named "Christ the King." Mother Mary also asked Charles to have people pray her rosary on this sacred ground.

Every day from 1947 to 1961, Mr. Grestl attended daily Mass. He was a devout Catholic. He had supernatural visions of Jesus, the Blessed Mother, St. Anne, St. Joseph, St. Michael, St. Peter, the Holy Spirit, and Our Heavenly Father. There were many more things that Charles saw, but he said, "There were too many to write down."

God the Father

Charles Grestl was born on November 22nd, 1885. His friends affectionately called him "Charlie". Besides working at the Oneida Knitting Mills, he was active in a number of youth groups. He was known as a regular guy, and a "walking saint" among his close friends. He never owned a car; he walked everywhere. He was a daily communicant at Our Lady of Lourdes Church in Utica. Today, this church has merged with Our Lady of the Rosary, and it has been renamed "Mary, Mother of Our Savior Church".

The Original Church – Our Lady of Lourdes in Utica, New York – Across from St. Elizabeth's Hospital on Genessee Street.

Other requests that were made during the 13 apparitions that Charles received were:

      1. Strike a medallion

2. Create a scapular with the same impression as the medallion on it. A scapular is a badge of membership in an order. It is usually worn over the shoulders.

Here is a scapular though the scapular would have the image of Christ the King and the Laborer

3. Pamphlets to be distributed all over the earth.

4. Pray the rosary at this site after approval of the shrine.

The site was consecrated by Monsignor Joseph May on June 14th, 1971. It thereby became holy ground. The Christ the King statue is at the apparition site. It is made from Carrara marble. Some of the fingers on the statue were broken. Now the statue is behind plexiglass.

Christ the King statue

The site was deeded to the Christ the King Foundation in 1972 and re-deeded to The Good News Foundation in 1999. With the hope and plan of a chapel being built, it will stand on its own. All are welcome here.

Saint Michael the Archangel – Charlie's Guardian Angel

At the age of 86, Charles Grestl died on November 21, 1972. He is buried in Forest Hill Cemetery in Utica, New York.

V

Christ the King Foundation

In 1973, 26 years after the first apparition, and two years after Charlie's death, Christ the King Foundation was established by a group of Utica area Catholics. Over the years, letters outlining Charles's apparitions have been sent to Pastor Father Collins, His Excellency, Bishop Walter Foery, His Eminence Francis Cardinal Spellman, and finally to His Holiness, Pope Pius the XII. In addition, a full account of his apparitions contained in a letter, were sent to His Holiness Pope

John XXIII dated March 8, 1961.

Senator James H. Donovan (1923 – 1990)

Also noteworthy, is that the late Senator James Donovan of Chadwicks, New York, has preserved Mr. Grestl's testimony on tape. He also was instrumental in acquiring the land where the apparitions took place through special legislation. Thus, a shrine was erected on the east side of Flanagan Road, one quarter of a mile from River Road off State Route 49 in the town of Marcy, New York.

St. Peter

Mr. Grestl testified that his first apparition took place on April 30, 1947. He was transported from the factory where he worked to a hillside off Flanagan Road in the town of Marcy, a community outside of Utica, New York. He began to walk, but soon found his way blocked by boulders, tree stumps and barbed wire. That was when he heard the voice say, "Hello son, come over here and sit down."

The Voice explained why his way was blocked. "Son, this is as far as you have gotten with your good works in life." That is when a bright light appeared, and Mr. Grestl was made aware that he was talking to Christ. Jesus told him to return home and continue his good works. In addition to youth groups, Mr. Grestl was also involved in church activities.

"Each time you come back; you will see the path cleared further upon the way to my Father's House." Our Lord spoke to him.

Charles Grestl was a mystic. He was a deeply pious man who was given a warning. He wrote a letter to Pope John XXIII regarding a warning that he received in regarding the danger to orphans and the failures of the clergy. 1

"The Son of Man shall send forth his angels, and they shall gather out of His kingdom all things that offend, and them which do iniquity; and shall cast them into a furnace of fire; there shall be a wailing and gnashing of teeth."
Matt. 13: 41-42

Saint Joseph

In one of the apparitions, Our Lord described to Charles the medal that he desired to be struck. It was to depict Christ Him and a laborer. Thus, both large and small medals have been cast by the Bliss Manufacturing Company of Attleboro, Massachusetts. The first ones, approximately thirty, were commissioned by Senator James Donovan in 1989. A gentleman by the name of Frank Zampardi, from Sauquoit, New York, designed the medal that was produced.

Medal designed by Frank Zampardi

A statue of Christ the King made from Carrara (Italian) marble, has been erected at this site.

Brochures were printed and distributed at various gatherings and parades.

Doris Goff, Mike Dziura, and Joe Rezpka

The Rosary is prayed in the morning on the various Holy days and public holidays at the Shrine. It is also recited on Thursday evenings in the summer led by Mike Dziura.

VI

The North American Martyrs

"The Blood of Martyrs is the Seed of Christians"

Tertullian

Eight Jesuit missionaries brought Jesus to the Indians of North American during the 17th Century. These Frenchmen met violent deaths while serving God and the church in remote parts of Eastern

Canada and New York state. They became known as the North American Martyrs.

Between the years of 1625 and 1649, the church raised these six priests and two Oblate laymen to sainthood as a result of their heroic missionary efforts. For spreading the Gospel, they were all murdered. In 1930, Pope Pius IX raised the group to sainthood.

There was John de Brebeuf, the first to arrive. He is known as the 'Apostle of the Hurons'. He witnessed thousands of baptisms in his 24 years of service. He even learned the Huron language making a dictionary that was very useful. However, in 1649, Brebeauf was captured along with his colleague Father Gabriel Lalemont by the marauding Iroquois.

The most horrific torture was executed on March 16th on Father de Brebeuf. The following day, likewise, was carried out on Father Lalemont. The Indians were astonished at the bravery of these holy men.

North American Martyrs – Auriesville, New York

Moreover, these Jesuits would beg for assignments to the most hardened of territories. Isaac Jogues and Rene Goupil. They were both captured by the Iroquois and tortured. When Father Rene was seen making the Sign of the Cross over a baby, he was immediately murdered by a tomahawk.

Father Jogues managed to escape, and he made his way back to New France being hailed as a hero. His biggest fear was that he would be unable to celebrate Mass as his fingers were badly mutilated by the Indians. However, Pope Urban VIII made a special exception for this courageous priest. Thus, on October 18th, 1946, Father Isaac

Jogues returned to New France where he met his martyrdom. While both he and Lalemont were trying to affect peace between the French, Hurons and Iroquois, they were blamed for a poor harvest.

Father Anthony Daniel was another one. He worked tirelessly teaching the faith to the Hurons at a seminary in Quebec. He also braved the elements going out in the wilderness teaching the Christian faith and baptizing native Canadians. He came back one night exhausted and having just finished celebrating Mass, an Iroquois war party attacked his mission at St. Joseph's. Father

Daniel was murdered. After being hit with a musket, he continued to give comfort, baptize and give absolution. Finally, a hatchet was taken to him.

Father Charles Garnier was also murdered the same year. He endured hunger, insults and deplorable living conditions yet he continued to perform his sacred ministry. With the constant threat of death looming, Father Garnier would continue to walk thirty miles a day regardless of heat or cold to spread the Gospel. He lived in squalor and filth ministering to the sick natives. he never counted the cost. On December 7, 1649, the Iroquois struck this man of God with a tomahawk. Heaven gained another saint.

Then, the next day, on the Feast of the Immaculate Conception, Father Noel Chabenel was returning to the Mission hub of Sainte Marie, Canada. One of the Hurons who converted under his instruction, killed him. Of all of these martyrs, Father Chabenel found it particularly difficult. He was not fond of the Indian culture. He did not master the language, and he was prone to depression. Despite this, Father Noel Chabenel took a vow to never forsake his missionary duties nor the anticipated martyrdom that was likely. He was the last of the eight Jesuits to die.

These heroic men filled with faith planted the seed of Christianity in bringing Jesus Christ into the world of the Indian. Their zeal, courage and willingness to sacrifice to the point where they laid down their lives to witness for Jesus is a shining star on the North American continent and in the church.

Only known portrait from life of "Catherine" Tekakwitha

c. 1690 by Father Chauchetiere

VII

Where Saints Have Trod and the Church Militant

Indeed, the Mohawk Valley is fertile soil where saints and many holy people have trod. Saint Kateri Tekakwitha, the Lily of the Mohawk, was born not far from here in Auriesville, New York in 1656. This area was known as Ossernenon then.   St. Isaac Jogues and his Jesuit missionary companions preached here. Kateri was an Algonquin-Mohawk Indian who converted to Catholicism at a young age having been so impressed by the Jesuits. She was heroic in her suffering and recognized for her strong Faith, and her kindness. [3]

Mother Marianne Cope, a canonized saint, grew up in Utica, New York. Her family immigrated from Germany in 1840 when she was just 2 years old.   Her family came from modest means. As a young adult, Marianne, then

Barbara Koob, worked in the factories of Utica. It was when she was accepted into the Order of Franciscan Sisters that Barbara took the name "Marianne".

One day, Mother Marianne received a letter to accept a position in a Hawaiian mission working with the lepers. She was already the supervisor of St. Joseph's Hospital in Syracuse.

She enthusiastically replied, "I am hungry for the work, and I wish with all my heart to be with the chosen ones, whose privilege it will be, to sacrifice themselves for the salvation of the souls of the poor Islanders... I am not afraid of any disease; hence it would be my greatest delight to minister to the abandoned lepers."

Mother Marianne's example – her never-failing optimism, her serenity, her caring nature, and her considerable abilities gave strength to the other Sisters.

Through devotion and self-sacrifice, the Sisters of Saint Francis rendered a remarkable service in the islands of Hawaii.

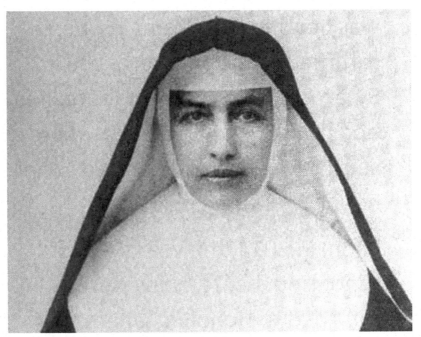
St. Mother Marianne Cope

St. Mother Marianne was never to return home. She died from natural causes at the age of 80 at Kalaupapa in 1918.

She was buried at the Bishop Home where she served.

However, in 2005, the year she was beatified, her remains were returned to the Motherhouse in Syracuse, New York. En route, her body was brought to Utica where a special Mass was celebrated in her honor. 4

Then, in 2014, the year she was canonized, her remains were returned to Honolulu where they are enshrined in the Cathedral Basilica of Our Lady of Peace.5

Many great things happen when praying at Christ the King Shrine. John Leary, a devout Catholic who has been attending daily Mass and receiving Holy Communion every day since he was 17 has spoken here. He also has received inner locutions from Our Blessed Mother on this site in addition to receiving daily messages from Our Lord and Mother Mary since his 1993 trip to Medjugorje. 2

John Leary – Prophet

Perhaps because the Utica area is a noted center for refugees. People have fled from war-torn countries to come here. They are hard-working immigrants from all over. They have come here with their Faith and strong family values. The Lord is close to them.

There is a lady named Elizabeth "Betty Frank" who received the Franciscan Peace Award by the Saint Kateri Tekakwitha Region of the Secular Franciscan Order.

Betty is the co-founder of the 24-hour Adoration Chapel at St. Joseph-St. Patrick Church in Utica.

Betty Frank, OFS, with her Peace Award in front of stained-glass window with

St. Mother Marianne Cope ministering to the sick

She has been an active supporter for Mother Marianne Cope's sainthood. She formed the Mother

Marianne Prayer Group and the Mother Marianne Shrine in Utica.

Elizabeth Frank is also the recipient of the "Pro Ecclesia et Pontifice" - the highest honor the Pope can bestow on a lay person.

Miss Frank is also a professed Secular Franciscan for almost 75 years promoting peace and justice. [7]

Betty Frank can also be found praying at the Christ the King Shrine when there are special devotions taking place.

Mary Jane Salatino (1925 – 2017)

Another wonderful lady who was Blessed with mystical gifts was the late Mary Jane Sacco Salatino. She held prayer meetings in her home. She raised a beautiful family. Having cancer, she suffered a lot albeit silently. She had a great devotion to Saint Therese, "The

Little Flower", who came down and tapped her knees. This relieved her tremendously resulting in a healing. [9]

Sister Mary Hope Therese Angeline, O. Carm – The Carmelite Sisters of the Aged and Infirm

The Mohawk Valley is fertile ground for God's Chosen Ones.

There is a sweet girl from West Winfield, New York. Her name is Dianna Hope Maring. Dianna was born January 13, 1987. This sweet soul professed her life to Our Lord in the Carmelite Order in Germantown, New York. In the eighth year of religious life, the Lord took Sister Mary Hope Therese Angeline, O. Carm to Himself six days after her 33rd birthday. Sister Mary Hope had a tender heart for the elderly whom she lovingly cared for as an occupational therapist. This precious child of God also was a gifted poet and like her religious name of St. Therese, she offered up all her sufferings. She underwent many surgeries and trials. Everyone whose life has been touched by Sister Mary Hope continues to be edified by her memory.

Sister Hope's mother is also a professed Third Order Carmelite, Sister Mary Joseph of John and the Holy Passion. She is a very holy and humble woman of God who has and continues to endure much. In March of 2022, her dear brother James Joseph suffered a stroke while caring for their mother. As a result, he was paralyzed from the neck down. Jo Ellen, like her brother, faithfully, offers it all up for the souls in purgatory.

d the Holy Passion

Sister Mary Joseph of John and the Holy Passion, O Carm.

Jo Ellen Maring

Three excerpts from Sister Mary Hope's poem:

'My Poem of Praise'

For good times and bad times in my life,

Times when only your love
would suffice,

For a chance to repent and to
forgive,

For the unique person that I
am,

As one with the sacrificial
Lamb.

Thank you, Lord, for a spirit
so tough,

That keeps me going when
things get rough,

For your gift to us in sacrifice,

For all that we have, you paid
the price.

Thank you for unconditional
love,

Inspiration from the Holy Dove,

And for graces you send from above.

Thank you, Dear Lord, your praises I sing,

I give thanks to you for everything. 10

Mike Dziura who has faithfully led the Holy Rosary for years in the Utica area leading the Rosary with Father Vincent Gigliotti

In January of 2000, Deacon John Joseph Droz, (1917 – 2009) conducted the first meeting of the Shrine with Alice M. Sunderlin, (1929 – 2021), a faithful lady with a great devotion to Our Lady. The Shrine was called "The Christ the

King Committee". It had been transferred to the Good News Foundation in 1999. Meetings were held monthly with Alice serving as the elected president.

Deacon John Joseph Droz and his wife Elizabeth Scheidelman Droz (Good News Foundation)

Deacon John Joseph Droz and his wife Elizabeth had a dream of planting the seeds of faith in the Mohawk Valley by evangelizing the hearts and minds of all to bring about a new springtime of Christianity. Through a generous endowment from Elizabeth Scheidelman Droz's parents, LeRoy and Hazel Scheidelman, the family were able to roll up their sleeves and begin The Good News Foundation which has been serving the Mohawk Valley for over twenty-five years. The mission has been to share the knowledge and love of Jesus Christ through hospitality, spiritual growth, and renewal, and support of individuals, parish communities and family life. A special emphasis is placed on strengthening marriages and families in the community.

Deacon John was a brilliant engineer and a family man raising nine children with his wife Elizabeth. He served in WWII as a 1st lieutenant flying over 50 missions over Germany. That he survived is a miracle in itself as he was a target as the Lead Navigator. In fact, no one in his plane was hurt, despite a 50% mortality rate. He developed refrigeration units;

did construction on a large scale and eventually had a real estate business, the largest in Central New York which he dedicated to Our Lord. For all his greatness and generosity, he was a humble man. He was a selfless man working with the youth, with urban renewal, traveling the world (over 70 countries) with his wife to further the love of Jesus Christ within the Catholic Church. They were always learning whether it was with Elderhostel or other classes to grow in the Faith. He along with Frank Winslow were the first deacons to be ordained in the city of Utica.

The Good News Foundation is 3.2 miles from Christ the King Shrine.

Dusk on Holy Ground

In 2009, the Shrine committee began an "Angel Garden" since Charles found Our Lord whittling an angel in his first apparition. There are other statues there too.

And like the Postal Workers, neither snow nor rain, nor heat, nor gloom of night stays these prayer warriors from their appointment with Christ the King

And the God of Peace be with you. Romans 15. God's Voice thunders in marvelous ways; He does great things beyond our understanding. He says to the snow, "Fall on the earth" and to the rain shower, "Be a mighty downpour" so that everyone He has made may know his work. Job 37:6

In December 2010, additional property was acquired through donations to the Committee.

The hand-carved steeple lovingly made by Father Madej

Front of the Shrine with the Celtic Cross walkway

A walkway formed in the shape of a Celtic cross has been completed after twenty-five years by local contractor Joseph Miller. Assisting Mr. Miller were Laborers from Local 35 and the Local 19 Unions along with four volunteers from the Youth Construction Program. It pleased Mr. Miller that the

Laborers got involved with a religious shrine that honors the Laborer. This was to fulfill the final request of the late Senator James Donovan.

Sketch of Proposed Shrine

A beautiful crucifix has been erected on the property too.

Crucifix in the back left along the road

Benches were donated by the local Boy Scouts.

Once the area was leveled, the Stations of the Cross were installed through a specific donation from Charles Grestl's nephew Bernard Grestl. The latter lived to be a centenarian (1917 – 2017). This was Bernard's memorial gift to honor his father Andrew Grestl who was a brother of Charles.

Bernard P. Grestl

Mass with Bishop Douglas Lucia from the Diocese of Syracuse at Holy Trinity Church in Utica, New York on the 75th Anniversary April 30, 2022

Fr. Gigliotti, Fr. Madej, Fr. Joseph Moskal, et al; Fr. Madej hand-carved the crown steeple for the Christ the King Chapel.

The mission of the Christ the King Shrine is to continue to implement the requests made to Charlie through the apparitions that he experienced.

Joseph Rezpka, Knight of Columbus, contractor who is working on the development of The Shrine Chapel

Today, and on the 75th anniversary of the apparitions of Charles Grestl, the shrine exists as a place "where all faiths can unite... for spiritual edification...to lift the hearts, minds and souls to spiritual things."

It is sweet to honor Christ the King

VIII

Christt the King

The title Christ the King represents Our Lord as the Divine King of the Universe. Christ is seated at the Right Hand of God the Father. I Corinthians 15:25 –28.

For (Christ) must reign until he has put all his enemies

under his feet. The last enemy to be destroyed is death. For God has put all things in subjection under his feet...when all things are subjected to him, then the Son himself will also be subjected to Him who put all things under him, that God may be all in all.

In 1925, Pope Pius XI instituted the Feast of Christ the King in response to a growing trend toward secularization, communism, and atheism. The Holy Father knew that we as Christians should make Our Lord first and foremost in every aspect of our lives.

We celebrate Christ's sovereignty on the 34th Sunday of the liturgical year, the last Sunday in Ordinary time. It is on the last Sunday before Lent which prefigures the end of history when Christ returns as King which is covered in the first half of Advent in the liturgies.

Pope Benedict the XVI has said that "The Kingship of Christ has remained completely hidden until he was thirty years old, years spent in an ordinary life in Nazareth. Then, during his public life, Jesus inaugurated the new kingdom "which does not belong to this world" (Jn 18:36), and finally, with his death and resurrection, he fully established it.

The Pope continues this reference in John 18:37...

"Pilate said to him, 'So you are a king?' Jesus answered, 'You say that I am a king. For this I was born, and for this I have come into the world, to bear witness to the truth. Everyone who bears witness to the truth hears my voice.'

Matthew 28:18

"And Jesus came and said to them, 'All authority in heaven and on earth has been given to me.'

Corinthians 15:25-28 and Philippians 2:10-11... *"At, the name of Jesus, every knee should bow, in heaven and on earth and under the earth, and every tongue confess that Jesus Christ is Lord, to the Glory of God the Father."*

"Oh, what happiness would be ours, if all men, individuals, families, and nations, would but let themselves be governed by Christ." Pope Pius XI

Pope Pius XI

Christ the King!

Bibliography

1. Bishop C. D. Timotheos – Apostolic See of Antioch
2. John Leary – the author can personally attest to this as she was present at the time and present on another occasion when this holy man prayed over her through his late son's intercession. The fruit of that prayer is a son born to M. Virginia Southworth at age 46 – 9 months from little David John Leary's entrance into Heaven.

3. www.Catholic.org>saints>St
4. National Park Service Hawaii – Nps.gov - Marianne Cope
5. The author had the honor of attending this Mass and praying through her intercession for a healthy maternity.
6. Mother Marianne Cope – Wikipedia
7. St. Joseph Fraternity newsletter posted by R. Stronach,OFS
8. Betty Franks has been given special "Lights" as the author witnessed on one such occasion at the Shrine. She was looking upward ecstatic

on the beauty and the colors that she was seeing.

9. The author is ever grateful for the prayers of Mrs. Salatino as a successful pregnancy ensued. She also received many messages from this holy lady as she had the gift of counsel. Mary Jane was also a dear friend to my Aunt Mary McDonald.

10.   Poems Reflections of Hope – Sr. M. Hope Therese Angeline Maring, O. Carm (2020 Carmelite Sisters of the Aged & Infirm)

11.   Cover – Bronze by

12.   St. Peter – photograph taken by Peter Paul Rubens

13. Photo credit John and Elizabeth Droz – Good News Foundation

14. Pictures of Christ the King Shrine – credit Peggy Goff Wilson, daughter of Doris B. Goff and great-niece of Charles Grestl, President of Christ the King Shrine

15. Author's note, my late brother Karl J. LaPointe died on the Feast of Christ the King in 1990. I would like to believe that Our Lord, Christ the King, has taken him unto Himself.

16. Cover – Joseph's Studio by Roman (Garden Statues, Heron)

17.   Pages 36-38 D.D. Emmons Catholic Simplicity

5/23

Made in USA - Kendallville, IN
34598_9798846419018
10.13.2022 1259